TAROT 2

Beginners' Guide on Real Tarot Card Meanings and How to Psychic Tarot Reading

Celestina Ortiz

Copyright © 2020 Celestina Ortiz

All rights reserved.

ISBN: 9798662778191

DEDICATION

The author and publisher have provided this e-book to you for your personal use only. You may not make this e-book publicly available in any way. Copyright infringement is against the law. If you believe the copy of this e-book you are reading infringes on the author's copyright, please notify the publisher at: https://us.macmillan.com/piracy

Contents

INTRODUCTION 1

THE REAL REASON PEOPLE BELIEVE IN ASTROLOGY AND TAROT CARD READINGS 3

CHAPTER 1: HOW TO GET STARTED 10

   I. 10 Top Decks To Consider When Buying Tarot Cards 10

   II. Which 2 Beginning Tarot Card Sets Are The Best, According To Reddit 17

   III. Tarot card meanings 20

CHAPTER 2: BEGINNERS' GUIDE 46

   I. 6 Step Study Guide 46

   II. Get tarot ready as beginner 65

CHAPTER 3: TAROT QUOTES 74

READY TO START YOUR TAROT JOURNEY? 80

INTRODUCTION

There's a lot of information out there if you're interested in reading the Tarot, and it can be a little overwhelming to sort through it all. This study guide will help you build a basic framework for your studies in the future. Topics include the history of Tarot, how to choose and care for a deck, the meanings of the cards themselves, and some basic spreads to try.

While there's no substitute for hands-on learning, this study guide is designed to give you many of the basic working concepts that you'll need to continue studying in earnest later on. Think of this as the foundation you can build onto in the future. Each lesson will feature four or five topics that you should read and study. Don't just skim over them -- read them thoroughly, and make notes on the points that jump out at you. Take your time when you're going through them, and if you need to, bookmark them to read later. In addition, each step has a simple "homework" assignment to try, so you can take the concepts you've read about, and see how they work in practice.

THE REAL REASON PEOPLE BELIEVE IN ASTROLOGY AND TAROT CARD READINGS

Is astrology real? And, doest tarot reading, horoscopes, and zodiac signs help us predict the future?

From an outside perspective, astrology and tarot cards may not be reliable sources for life advice, but for some people, it's a harmless way to seek answers for their problems.

But, unless you did it as part of a parlor game, when you tell most people that you've consulted an astrologer or had a tarot reading, you're likely to get a lot of funny looks.

You might even get a lecture from a born-again Christian about how sinful these things are and that you might wind up in Hell.

At the very least, you're likely to hear the argument about how these things have been scientifically disproven and how many practitioners of these disciplines are charlatans.

My response to these: Who cares? It doesn't matter

Most of the time, people who seek out occult practitioners for advice are in some kind of crisis. That's just when they need to do some serious critical thinking about a situation in their lives that's causing them a lot of pain.

I once did exactly this and I found astrology and tarot so helpful to me that I started studying both disciplines.

"But astrology and tarot card readings can't actually predict the future!" many will protest.

That's exactly right and as a student astrologer, I can tell you why: because you have the power of choice in your life. When I look at your astrology chart, if I look at a long enough span of time, I see the main spheres of endeavor your life is about and I can see the choice points you have and how those can work out later on.

All of the choice points and possible outcomes are there, though they can be difficult to disentangle.

Sometimes you have a very heavy probability of choosing

this path or that, but astrology is never going to tell you your future. (And, therefore, neither am I.)

That's because the planets aren't making the choices. You are.

Where disciplines like astrology, tarot, horoscopes, zodiac signs, and runes do their magic is in their description of your situation.

Once upon a time, I suffered a very painful breakup. I found this online tarot site and every time I did a reading, the cards just screamed at me. I was too controlling, they said. I was too domineering, they said. I was too needy, they said, and I really needed to work on that. This hurt and baffled me, because it was a three-party situation. From what I was given to understand, I was a kitten compared to the other woman. That was her the cards were describing, not me!

Here, however, is where divination has its value: When you

sit there staring at the cards and going, "I'm not like that! How could this possibly be the truth?"

When you start combing through the possibilities as "If what you're being told were true," that is when you gain in wisdom from the cards. Or the stars. Or the runes.

Over time, through my tears, I began to see that I was, in fact, thinking and about to behave toward this man the same way the other woman had. In a much milder degree, but there it was.

These weren't good traits to have and if we'd stayed together, I would have ended up treating him just the same as she did!

I know this, not because the cards said so, but because I looked critically at what I was thinking during the relationship, how I expected him to act, how I expected we'd live, what I expected we'd do.

How did that square with my conscience, given what I

knew about how this person had already been treated? Was I being needy and domineering, or not?

Uh-oh. Sometimes the truth hurts.

Then I had to think to myself, "Why was I doing that? How could I treat someone whom I loved that way?"

Astrology had something to say to me about that, too. Your natal chart comments a lot on how you were raised and how your childhood affects the person you are today.

Reflecting on that, I saw some things I had sort of shrugged off to the side, especially about how my father treated me when I was young. He passed away when I was only 12 years old, and I'd spent so long without him, I didn't think what happened before then was important.

What matters here is not that the astrology said it was important, but that it made me think about it. It made me consider whether I believed it was important or not.

If I disagreed, why? If I agreed, why? What should I do

about that?

As another example, as the child of a mentally ill mother, I have read enough about codependency that I recognize it when I see it in a horoscope chart.

My charts with the fellow in question warned that the relationship would be heavily codependent, and forecasted, more and more as the relationship went on, emotional dishonesty in the relationship, cheating, and a devastating breakup.

It didn't have to go that way, but it was most likely that it would.

I certainly wasn't happy to see that. But, because of my background, I was able to lay hands on more reading about codependency than just Codependent No More, the seminal Melody Beattie book from the eighties.

That was when I discovered not only that severely enmeshed codependent relationships often end in exactly the way our charts described, but why.

Oh, and that showed up in our transits, too. With the additional information I had, I could see this was going to be the truth if I were with this guy and nobody got well from childhood.

Again, I could consider: "Do I want to be this codependent? Do I want somebody who is, and who won't work on his problems? How would I feel if all this actually happened in the future?

If the guy comes back, he has some codependency recovery work to do. If he doesn't do it, I need to ease on down, ease on down the road.

It's been a very in-depth study, but I can definitely say I've profited from it. I will never be so naive and idealistic about people who look healthier than I am, ever again.

It is in the thinking and consideration of the possibilities occultism and divination bring up that we become wise.

CHAPTER 1: HOW TO GET STARTED

I.10 Top Decks To Consider When Buying Tarot Cards

1. Rider-Waite Tarot Deck

This deck has 78 cards and was originally published in 1909 and is considered the gold standard for tarot decks, most decks are modeled from this deck. A Great beginner deck, there is plenty of information about how to use this deck available.

The deck contains highly symbolic artwork but is pretty basic in artistic design. Easy use to use and sold in many locations and platforms.

2. New Age Gilded Tarot Deck

The Gilded Tarot deck is a 78 card deck by artist Ciro Marchetti. This is a beautiful fantasy deck incorporating medieval, and even steampunk design elements.

The artist used both hand-drawn and digital designs to create this fantastic and beautifully colored deck. This deck is a vibrant deck modeled off the traditional Rider-Waite symbolism and would make certainly a lovely choice.

3. Renaissance Tarot Deck

This lovely deck of 78 cards created by artist Brian Williams, uses Greek god and goddess type figures as well as mythology scenes to portray the symbolism of tarot. Each card takes an opportunity to touch upon the stories and themes of ancient mythology.

With golden touches through the deck, its bound to be entrancing to use. The subtle colors and design style reminiscent of the historical art style of the Renaissance time period. Having this deck could feel like owning art you could have seen in a museum of ancient works.

4. Dreams Of Gaia Tarot Deck

The Dreams of Gaia deck contains 81 cards by artist

Ravynne Phelan, each card is an artistic design dream, with colors combined in strong and vibrant detail. The colors used allow the cards each embody a bold symbolic statement.

Every card in this deck is beyond beautiful and I adore the nature theme throughout the deck, I really feel a connection to using Tarot in this way. If this deck connects with you, I think you would love it so much you may not ever want to use another.

5. *Good Tarot Deck*

This is a 78 card deck. The cards in this beautiful deck are ethereal and delicate. A fairytale feel to each card with soft flowing colors and lovely card designs.

I like the energy of this deck because it offers a positive vibe to all the cards, no negative approach to these cards, instead it offers positive feedback even to tricky situations.

These cards have dreamy psychic imagery and symbols

rooted in ancient times. The cards have a simple vibe and offer growth centered interpretations.

6. Crystal Visions Tarot Deck

Crystal Visions is a deck by artist Jennifer Galasso and has 79 cards. This dreamy deck was named for Stevie Nick's album "Crystal Visions". This deck has an unknown "blank" type card to indicate an unknowable element when drawn.

The Crystal Visions deck is based off the Raider Waite deck, using exquisitely beautiful card designs to convey the energy and symbols of tarot. The images are straightforward and clean designs.

The figures in the cards, while beautifully drawn, are bold and as tarot should be, symbolically full. For instance, the Death card has Rider-Waite symbols and others such as runes and the Egyptian ankh.

7. Cosmic Tarot Deck

The Cosmic Tarot is a 78 card deck created by artist Norbert Losche. I have to say this is the next deck on my personal list, I intended to have this set one day soon. I found it about a year ago on Pinterest and have seen them in a local shop more recently.

I was struck by both the images and energy of this cosmically beautiful deck. To me, it has an art deco theme which I have a soft spot for anyway.

The dignity in these cards is evident to me. I love the colors used, while muted they are still intense. Definitely a deck for wrapping in a silk scarf.

8. Vice Versa Tarot Deck

The Vice Versa Tarot deck by two artists' Massimiliano Filadoro, and Davide Corsi. This is a deck I plan to have, and it promises to be an exciting event once I do. This is a very unique deck, it is comprised of 78 cards but every card has a fully designed backside, a reflection image of the front, for a total of 156 images.

Alternate meanings are included in the guidebook. I wouldn't call this a beginner deck, but if you love them, remember you don't have to have a standard starting point if you have the passion to understand them, and to definitely mention the artwork will be there to fuel your excitement along the way.

9. *ShadowScapes Tarot Deck*

ShadowScapes Tarot Deck was created by artist Stephanie Pui-Mun Law. There are 78 cards in this stunning deck. I own this particular deck, a gift from my mom. This deck is splendid with heavenly watercolor images.

This deck also focuses on positive energy and the companion book is loaded with 78 ephemeral stories to go with each card, a deep lesson lies in each story. I have loved using these cards and my readings have been very insightful, the perspective I am able to gain from them is notable for my experience.

10. *Wild Unknown Tarot Deck*

The Wild Unknown Tarot Deck is a 78 card deck by artist Kim Krans. This is a really cool deck of cards. Themed like the Gaia deck with nature as the prominent symbols, instead of painted or colored images these cards are more similar to hand-drawn sketches with vibrant pops of color in each giving emphasis to the colored portion.

The Wild Unknown is a very popular deck and the tarot cards are easy to understand. The companion book is 207 pages of detail on understanding the animal totem symbols in each card.

II. Which 2 Beginning Tarot Card Sets Are The Best, According To Reddit

1. *Highest amount of points response:*

"If you're just starting out, I'd stick with the Rider-Waite deck and the Celtic Cross spread. Then, when you start to feel more confident in your abilities you can look around for a pack which 'speaks' to you, and try different spreads."

Exploring Tarot Using Radiant Rider-waite Tarot: Deck Book Set, Amazon.com

This all-inclusive set seems ideal for beginners as it comes with a book to explain everything AND a set of cards to get started. Plus, it has illustrations! I don't know about you, but when I'm learning a new skill, I adore an illustration to help me fully understand a concept. Personally, this would be the one I would go with if you want to start learning about Tarot cards!

The Celtic Cross Tarot Spread: Cutting to the Chase,

Amazon.com

This one seems ideal if you want to learn, but you have less time to commit to learning the practice since this one advertises as "no muss no fuss". While it doesn't look like this one comes with cards (so, you'll have to purchase those separately), it seems like this one gets right into the fun of the readings without a lot of "how to" reading. I'm thinking this is good for those who just want to play and not learn the ins and outs of the Tarot.

2. Second highest amount of points response:

"I purposely study using the Thoth deck and it's accompanying book "The Book of Thoth" by Aleister Crowley (he may have a reputation, but he knew his stuff)."
Are you a fan of astrology? Then this could be the deck for you as it contains astrological attributes and comes with instructions for use. This deck may be a bit of a pricier route though as it looks like you get the most value out of

this if you buy the book, The Book Of Thoth, to go with it (the book can be found below).

Accompanying Book - "The Book of Thoth"

The Book of Thoth: A Short Essay on the Tarot of the Egyptians, Amazon.com

For those interested in more of the historical aspects of Tarot cards readings, this could be the best route for you. This book delves into the study of the Egyptian tarot and pairs great with the above Thoth deck (found above).

Nicole Bradley-Bernard is a writer who needs coffee more than she needs anyone's approval. She enjoys putting bright colors in her curly brown hair, spending time outside on cool days and being with her partner in life, Eric, who she considers a continuing source of inspiration.

III. Tarot card meanings

THE FOOL

A new phase of life begins, a risk must be taken,

a need to abandon the old and start something new. New experiences, personal growth, development. The discovery of talents.

THE MAGICIAN

A person or possibilities. New skills are available, potential is growing, opportunities and adventures unfolding.

Success in everything by utilising the skills, tools and resources that are available.

THE EMPRESS

The Mother of fertility and growth. New things about to enter a situation,

there may be a birth coming or a new path in life. Marriage

/ Relationship / Pregnancy / Patience / Motherhood.

THE EMPEROR

A need to make something solid, to solidify an idea, to build something with a firm structure. Authority / Control / Dominance. Man of power, an employer or a domineering male.

THE HIGH PRIESTESS

A time for reflection, allowing secrets to be revealed, showing potential abundance as yet unfulfilled. Pay attention to your dreams and intuition. Where the magician is all about possibilities, the High Priestess is all about truly understanding those possibilities.

THE HIEROPHANT

Need for spiritual purpose, the search for a personal philosophy. Increased studying and learning.

Humility/Teaching/Getting through deeply frightening and difficult situations.

This card can sometimes suggest marriage or a serious turn towards religion.

THE LOVERS

A love affair with a trial or choice attached.

This card indicates that these decisions or choices are incredibly important and significant so it is essential that you choose the right path. True partnership. The card is all about choices, intuitively rather than by the use of intellect.

CHARIOT

Conflict within / Struggles and battles / Potential for victory / Resolution of quarrels / Moving forward / Overcoming opposition through confidence / Control and Determination / Trip.

JUSTICE

Need for clarity of mind, impartial judgement and a balanced intellect. Legal matters needing attention (marriage license, divorce decree, financial arrangement). The fairest decision
will be made. You are being called to account for your actions and will be judged accordingly.

TEMPERANCE:

Harmony within relationships. Happy marriage or partnership. Adaptation, coordination and tempering external influences.
Balance / Patience / Moderation.

STRENGTH

Facing the things or the truth in a situation that you have been putting off for too long. Overcoming your fears.

Courage / Inner Will / Optimism.

THE HERMIT

A time for withdrawal, silent meditation and solitude. Patience is needed to confront one's inner world. Could be someone who likes to or needs to work alone.

THE WHEEL OF FORTUNE

Change in fortune, new beginnings, a new chapter in life starting. The Wheel makes a new turn. Remain optimistic and have faith in the Universe that it will take care of the situation.

THE HANGED MAN

Sacrifice must be made to gain something of greater value. It is all about waiting, in order to allow new possibilities to arise. Vulnerability

/ Selflessness / New Perspectives. A willingness to adapt to changed circumstances

is the main theme of this card.

DEATH

The most misunderstood card in the deck. The end of something which has been lived out, transformation, new beginnings to follow. Death indicates a time of significant change and transition.

THE DEVIL

A confrontation with the inner world. Facing fears and inhibitions can foster growth. The Devil reflects actual addictions and dependencies in your life, such as alcoholism, drug-taking, unhealthy relationships, over-spending., etc. Breaking

of habits and ceasing to dance to the devil's tune.

THE TOWER

Breaking down existing forms, changing false structures and finding true values. Change around the home or emotionally challenging periods - a time of great upheaval. It symbolizes conflict and overall disruption of life, but for the greater good.

It's about facing things you have been reluctant

THE STAR

to deal with. It could lead to good or bad things, but this action needs to done.

THE MOON

Time of passivity rather than action.

The Moon is a card of psychic forces,

so let go of your conscious mental blocks

and allow your intuition to guide you.

Optimism, time of passive action, energy

THE SUN

in abundance, a time of clear vision.

It is about embracing your destiny and giving

it everything you have got. Happiness / Success / Good health. This card relates to achievement, at work or through studies. Travel to a warm or tropical climate.

Time for reaping rewards for past actions,

JUDGEMENT

and reaching conclusions. You have reviewed and evaluated your past experiences and have learned from them. "Rebirth" or renewal

of the self, changes to the better: getting well after a long sickness, or finding a new career or spiritual path.

Success, achievement, attainment,

THE WORLD

the realization of a goal or the completion of a cycle. This card can indicate world travel. Feeling of being welcome anywhere you go.

THE MINOR ARCANA

The Minor Arcana (Including the Court Cards

The Minor Arcana: (covering preoccupations, activities and emotions) highlights the more practical aspects of life and can refer to current issues that have a temporary or minor influence.

If a Tarot reading is predominantly made up of the Minor Arcana Tarot cards, you are dealing with issues which will not necessarily having a lasting influence on your life.

The Court Cards: Within the Minor Arcana are the Court Cards - Page, Knight, Queen and King. These cards most often represent people: ourselves, our thoughts, people in our lives and personalities, a level of maturity. They may relate to behaviour or situations in some cases. PAGES conceive ideas, KNIGHTS act upon ideas, QUEENS nurture ideas and KINGS develop ideas to an established and stable state.

ACE OF CUPS

Upsurge of feelings and emotion, new relationships. Love affair, the birth of a child.

TWO OF CUPS

Commitment to romance, partnership or friendship (early days, "blind love").

THREE OF CUPS

Celebration. A stage for rejoicing.

The commitment to a future has been made.

FOUR OF CUPS

Self-absorbed. Content with things as they are.

Unwilling to be moved from this portion.

FIVE OF CUPS

Regret over past actions, loss or betrayal in love.

Separation, but all is not lost.

SIX OF CUPS

Past effort may bring present rewards or an old lover may reappear. Sentimental time.

SEVEN OF CUPS

A choice to be made with many options open.

Careful decisions must be made. Act. There is a risk of illusion. You need to avoid escapism protect yourself against unclear thinking.

Leaving past behind. Letting go,

EIGHT OF CUPS

no matter how much energy has been put into something.

Walk away. Follow your dream card.

A wish of paramount importance will come true.

NINE OF CUPS

Great emotional joy.

Happiness and contentment, with a sense

TEN OF CUPS

of permanence and future purpose.

It often suggests starting a family.

The sense of harmony.

PAGE OF CUPS

in the world of emotion. "New Phase"-

birth of a child, new relationship, engagement. Show your feelings; listen to your inner voice. Take a fresh perspective on a difficult issue and approach that situation with benefit of the doubt and love.

Spirit of romance. A gentle, caring lover

KNIGHT OF CUPS

and friend. Sensitive and affectionate. Thoughtful. Chivalrous. Creative and artistic.

The Knight of Cups may suggest a proposal is coming.

A person who possesses a strong perceptive nature

QUEEN OF CUPS

and deep desire to learn about the inner world.

Mature Female. Follow your heart.

Peace and Harmony. Go with the flow.

Meeting with caring, concerned, nurturing

KING OF CUPS

person or it may be that you have to develop some of the maternal, protective qualities within yourself. Emotional balance.

THE WANDS CARDS

ACE OF WANDS

An upsurge of creative energy, drive and energy.

Great potential for success.

TWO OF WANDS

Intuitive choice. Two possibilities, equally good.

Firm plans must be formulated.

THREE OF WANDS

A stage of initial completion of a creative project. New ideas forming. New forces of energy being generated.

FOUR OF WANDS

A time to pause for celebration after hard efforts (holiday, period of rest and relaxation). "The Marriage Card".

FIVE OF WANDS

A time of struggle, petty obstacles constantly appear and cause difficulties. Open conflict. Certain issues cause a lot of tension and confusion.

SIX OF WANDS

Public acclaim, promotion, recognition for work and effort (winning a scholarship, gaining

a qualification, getting a lead role, publishing a book or success in any other chosen field).

SEVEN OF WANDS

The stage after the public recognition. Stiff competition must now be faced. Hold you ground. Renewed determination and courage are necessary.

EIGHT OF WANDS

A period of fruitful progress after a delay or struggle. Everything is on your side.

NINE OF WANDS

Strength in reserve can provide enough energy to win the battle, although resources seem exhausted. Push hard.

TEN OF WANDS

There is danger implied in taking on more than one can cope with. Inadequate awareness of our limitations.

PAGE OF WANDS

The bearer of good news, a desire or stirring of creative growth. Free spirit. Follow creative urges, be spontaneous. "New Phase" in which your cre-ative world must be developed.

KNIGHT OF WANDS

Spirit of Adventure, move of home or country. Exciting and unreliable young man. Time to develop exuberant and adventurous qualities. Passionate, spontaneous.

QUEEN OF WANDS

The person embodying creative, imaginative and intuitive

powers or through development

of these qualities within yourself. Strong Leader. Ex-ercise, be active. Social Network.

The Queen of Wands' characteristics often lead to the performing arts.

KING OF WANDS

Meeting a fiery, impulsive, enthusiastic person or it may mean that you yourself will have

to develop some of the optimism and exuberance he possesses. Creative power. He enjoys starting new projects, but does not always finish up.

THE SWORDS CARDS

ACE OF SWORDS

Inevitable and irrevocable change. Awakening of mental

powers which may cause conflict at first but are ultimately conducive to growth and development.

FOUR OF SWORDS

A need for rest or retreat after stress, a time for convalescence after tension.

FIVE OF SWORDS

Pride must be swallowed, limitations accepted, be-fore further progress can be made. We have to work within the framework of that situation.

SIX OF SWORDS

A card of harmony. A period of calm after great anx-iety, release of tension, a peaceful journey towards smoother waters (sometimes physical move away from unpleasant surroundings).

SEVEN OF SWORDS

A need for evasion and avoidance of direct confrontation in order to achieve objective. Use brain, tact, diplomacy, rather than brawn and aggression

EIGHT OF SWORDS

A fear of moving out of a situation of bondage, paralysis. (Indicates a situation of tension

similar to Two of Swords. In this case, however, the choices are perfectly conscious).

NINE OF SWORDS

A time in which the mind is tormented by fears

of impending doom. Nightmares and fantasies trouble the mind, even though the facts do not match the fears.

TEN OF SWORDS

The end of a painful situation or state. There emerges an ability to see a situation realistically. Once something is ended, the way is cleared for a fresh start. Clear break.

PAGE OF SWORDS

"New Phase", mentally active period. Go for it. Beginnings of intellectual development; gossip or idle talk may cause disruption.

KNIGHT OF SWORDS

Time of communication and mental development, new idea or vision. Mind-expanding, progressive period. Great ambition, determination and strength to succeed no matter what.

QUEEN OF SWORDS

The sternness of a mature intellect which is devoid of emotion. Difficult decisions. Keep clear head, be independent in thought and judgement. Use facts and logic. Face up to the truth.

Don't let yourself be fooled.

KING OF SWORDS

Meeting an intelligent and charming,

high principled person. Symbol of intellectual power and authority. Professional advisor. Develop logic and reasoning powers.

PENTACLES

ACE OF PENTACLES

Material achievement is possible, financial aid may be available for the beginning of new enterprise.

TWO OF PENTACLES

Change and fluctuation in financial matters, but harmony within the change. An optimism and enthusiasm which balances out anxieties about fi-nancial affairs. Finances, luck.

THREE OF PENTACLES

A satisfactory time. Initial completion of work, a basic structure is built which still requires the finishing touches.

FOUR OF PENTACLES

There is danger in clinging too tightly to what one has earned. Nothing is lost, but nothing can be gained. Miserliness (usually money) can be extended to the realm of feelings.

FIVE OF PENTACLES

Financial loss and hardship. Loss of luck / health. Loss on a deeper level; of esteem, of faith in oneself / life.

SIX OF PENTACLES

Help from a generous friend or employer, a situation in which there is money or good fortune to be shared.

SEVEN OF PENTACLES

A difficult decision must be made, between material security and uncertain new opportunities. This is a card about patience and letting things ripen.

EIGHT OF PENTACLES

The apprentice, training or starting out anew in another profession.

NINE OF PENTACLES

A card of great satisfaction and pleasure, reward for effort, material benefits.

TEN OF PENTACLES

Financial stability and foundation for home and family.

PAGE OF PENTACLES

Beginning awareness of the value of material sense; slow development. Consider further study. Start saving money for future. Apply careful planning in order to manifest your dreams and achieve your goals.

You need to remain focused on the practical and tangible elements.

KNIGHT OF PENTACLES

Spirit of determination and earthy practicality is due to enter your life. A person of integrity. Some-one who can be counted on.

QUEEN OF PENTACLES

Represents prosperity and security. Meeting with an affectionate, generous, sensuous person. Mother figure. Finances are definitely improving, business success. Take a sensible approach, be resourceful and practical. Maintain "down to earth" attitude. Create balance.

KING OF PENTACLES

Meeting wealthy, ambitious, materially-oriented per-son or you may need to develop some drive for ma-terial gain within.

CHAPTER 2: BEGINNERS' GUIDE

Tarot has long been met with superstition and was once seen as the preserve of hippies with a fondness for the occult and chintzy fortune teller stereotypes. Now, the art of reading the tarot is back in style. With people reaching for the cards more than ever before and general sales of decks at the highest they have been in 50 years, tarot cards are experiencing a huge, almost cultish following.

Although tarot is becoming more mainstream, it can still seem intangible and confusing. What is tarot, where does it come from and what do the cards mean? Don't panic! Tarot fundamentals are easy to understand. We've broken down everything a beginner should know. So, if you're curious about where you should start, this ultimate tarot beginners guide should help you out.

1.6 Step Study Guide

Step 1: Getting Started in Tarot

Welcome to the step in your Intro to Tarot study guide - let's go ahead and get started! We're going to begin with a look at the basics of Tarot -- and even if you think you know Tarot, you should go ahead and read this anyway. We'll also discuss how to select and care for a deck of cards.

A Brief History of Tarot

Tarot cards have been around for several centuries, but they were originally an entertaining parlor game, rather than a tool of divination. Find out what changed, and why Tarot became one of our most popular divination methods.

Tarot 101: A Basic Overview

What is Tarot? To people unfamiliar with divination, it may seem that someone who reads Tarot cards is "predicting the future." However, most Tarot card readers will tell you that the cards offer a guideline, and the reader is simply interpreting the probable outcome based on the forces presently at work.

Selecting Your Tarot Deck

For a beginning Tarot reader, few tasks are as daunting as actually choosing that first deck. There are hundreds of different Tarot decks available. Really, it can be a little overwhelming. Here are some tips on selecting the deck that works best for you.

Keeping Your Cards Safe

So you've finally found the deck of Tarot cards that speaks to you -- congratulations! You've brought them home... but now what do you do with them? Learn how to "charge" your cards, and protect them from both physical damage and negative energy.

Exercise: Explore Different Decks

So are you ready for your first homework assignment?

We'll have one at the end of each step, and this first one is a fun one. Your exercise for today - or however long you want to spend on it - is to go out and look at different Tarot decks. Ask friends if you can see theirs, go to bookstores and peek at the boxes, dig around at the local Wiccan Shoppe if you have one nearby. Get a feel for all the different decks that are available to you. If you find one you like enough to buy, that's great, but if you don't, that's okay too - your deck will come to you when you're ready.

Step 2: Get Ready to Read the Cards

So how, exactly, do you do a Tarot reading? Well, for starters, you'll want to prepare your deck -- and yourself -- before you get going. We'll also look at different things you'll need to know about interpreting the cards themselves. Finally, we'll dig right into the first group of cards in the Major Arcana!

How to Prepare for a Tarot Reading

So you've got your Tarot deck, you've figured out how to keep it safe from negativity, and now you're ready to read for someone else. Let's talk about the things you should do before you take on the responsibility of reading cards for another person.

Interpreting the Cards

Now that you've laid down your Tarot cards, this is where the real fun begins. If someone has come to you as a Querent, it's because they want to know what's going on -- but they also want it to be interesting. After all, anyone can flip open a book and read that the Ten of Cups means contentment and happiness. What they really want to know is how does it apply to them, specifically?

The Major Arcana, Part 1

Cards 0 - 7: The Material World

Within the Major Arcana, there are three distinct groups of cards, each representing a different aspect of the human experience. The first set, Cards 0 - 7, reflect issues pertaining to the material world - situations related to job success, education, finances, and marriage. The 0 Card, the Fool, begins his journey through life and travels the road throughout the cards. As he does, he learns and grows as a person.

0 - The Fool

1 - The Magician

2 - The High Priestess

3 - The Empress

4 - The Emperor

5 - The Hierophant

6 - The Lovers

7 - The Chariot

Exercise: A Single Card

For this exercise, we're going to keep things very basic. Set aside the eight cards referenced above. Take some time to get to know their meanings, both forward and reversed. Each day, before you do anything else, draw one of these cards at random. As your day progresses, take some time to reflect on how the day's events connect and relate to the card you drew in the morning. You may want to keep a journal of which cards you draw, and what happens throughout the day. Also, at the end of a week, look back and see if one card has appeared more often than others. What do you think it's trying to tell you?

Step 3: The Major Arcana, Part 2

In the previous lesson, your exercise was to draw one card each day out of the first eight cards of the Major Arcana. How did you do? Did you notice any patterns, or were all your results random? Was there a particular card that stood out to you?

Today, we're going to delve a bit further into the Major Arcana, and we're also going to look at the suits of

Pentacles/Coins and Wands. We'll also expand on the previous step's daily card exercise.

The Major Arcana, Part 2:

Cards 8 - 14: The Intuitive Mind

While the first section of the Major Arcana deal with our interactions in the material world, the second group of cards focuses more on the individual being, rather than societal issues. Cards 8 - 14 are based on how we feel, instead of what we do or think. These cards are attuned to the needs of our hearts, as well as our search for faith and truth. It should be noted that in some decks, Card 8, Strength, and Card 11, Justice, are in opposite positions.

8 - Strength

9 - The Hermit

10 - The Wheel of Fortune

11 - Justice

12 - The Hanged Man

13 - Death

14 - Temperance

The Suit of Pentacles/Coins

In the Tarot, the suit of Pentacles (often portrayed as Coins) is associated with matters of security, stability and wealth. It's also connected to the element of earth, and subsequently, the direction of North. This suit is where you'll find cards that relate to job security, educational growth, investments, home, money and wealth.

The Suit of Wands

In the Tarot, the suit of Wands is associated with matters of intuition, wit, and thought processes. It's also connected to the element of fire, and subsequently, the direction of South. This suit is where you'll find cards that relate to creativity, communication with others, and physical activity.

Exercise: A Three Card Layout

Last time, you drew a single card each day. You may have

noticed some trends and patterns. Now, add the second batch of Major Arcana cards into your pile, as well as the Wands and Pentacles. Shuffle them every morning, and repeat the previous exercise -- only this time, you'll draw three cards each morning, rather than just one. Look at all three as not just individual cards, but as parts of a whole. How do they fit together? Do two of them seem closely related while the third seems unconnected? Write down each card that you've drawn, and as the day goes on, see if events bring the cards to mind. You may be surprised when you look back on your day!

Step 4: The Major Arcana, Part 3

In the previous step, you drew three cards each day, using the first two-thirds of the Major Arcana, and the suits of Wands and Pentacles. By now, you should be getting a good feel for the symbolism behind the different cards. Are you seeing trends in the cards you pull every morning? Be sure to keep track of what cards you get, and note whether they reveal anything to you throughout the day.

This time, we'll finish up the Major Arcana, and we'll look at the two other suits, Cups and Swords.

The Major Arcana, Part 3:

Cards 15 - 21: The Realm of Change

Within the Major Arcana, so far we've talked about the first third of the cards which deal with our interactions in the material world. The next group involves our intuitive mind and our feelings. This final group of cards in the Major Arcana, cards 15 - 21, deal with universal laws and issues. They go far beyond the feelings of the individual and the needs of society. These cards address circumstances that can forever alter our lives and the path upon which we travel.

15 - The Devil

16 - The Tower

17 - The Star

18 - The Moon

19 - The Sun

20 - Judgment

21 - The World

The Suit of Swords

The suit of Swords is associated with matters of conflict, both physical and moral. It's also connected to the element of air, and subsequently, the direction of East. This suit is where you'll find cards that relate to conflict and discord,

The Suit of Cups

The suit of Cups is associated with matters of relationships and emotions. As you may expect, it's also connected to the element of water, and subsequently, the direction of West. It's where you'll find cards that relate to love and heartbreak, choices and decisions related to emotion, family situations, and anything else that connects to how we interact with the people in our lives.

Exercise: A Five Card Layout

Last time we used about half of the deck to draw three cards. For this step, your assignment is to use the entire deck, and pull five cards each day before you do anything else. Figure out how they apply to the events of the day, your needs and desires, and the environment surrounding you. Do you notice a certain suit appearing more often than others? Is there a trend towards Major Arcana cards?

Step 5: Tarot Spreads

By now you should be feeling pretty comfortable with the idea of looking at a card and figuring out not only its meaning but how it applies to you. After all, you've been pulling cards each day, right? Have you noticed that one card keeps appearing more than others? Is there a trend towards a certain number or suit?

Now we're going to work on three very simple spreads that

you can try, which are perfect for beginners, and will help you look at different aspects of a question. If we look at Tarot cards as a tool of guidance, rather than just "fortune telling," we can use them to evaluate a situation to decide on the right course of action.

The Pentagram Spread

The pentagram is a five-pointed star sacred to many Pagans and Wiccans, and within this magical symbol, you'll find a number of different meanings. Within the pentagram, each of the five points has a meaning. They symbolize the four classical elements -- Earth, Air, Fire, and Water -- as well as Spirit, which is sometimes referred to as the fifth element. Each of these aspects is incorporated into this Tarot card layout.

The Romany Spread

The Romany Tarot spread is a simple one, and yet it reveals a surprising amount of information. This is a good spread to use if you are just looking for a general overview of a situation, or if you have several different interconnected issues that you're trying to resolve. This is a fairly free-form spread, which leaves a lot of room for flexibility in your interpretations.

One of the most popular spreads in use today is the Seven Card Horseshoe spread. Although it utilizes seven different cards, it's actually a fairly basic spread. Each card is positioned in a way that connects to different aspects of the problem or situation at hand.

Exercise: Practice a Layout

Your homework assignment is to practice these three layouts - try each of them at least once. Use them to read for yourself every day -- and if possible, try to read for someone else. If you're worried that you'll get things "wrong," don't panic. Ask a good friend or trusted family member to let you read for them, using one of the above spreads. Let them know you need some practice, and ask them to give you honest feedback about how you're doing.

Step 6: More About the Tarot

After the previous lesson, you should have spent some time working with the Pentagram layout, the Seven Card Horseshoe, and the Romany spread. How did you do? Did you get a chance to read for someone else? Are you feeling more comfortable with the interpretations of the cards?

In this step, we'll wrap things up with the fairly detailed Celtic Cross spread. We'll also talk about those rare occasions where a Tarot reading just doesn't work - and what to do when it happens - as well as the question of whether the moon phase matters in Tarot and finally, how you can use Tarot cards in spellwork.

The Celtic Cross

The Tarot layout known as the Celtic Cross is one of the most detailed and complex spreads used. It's a good one to use when you have a specific question that needs to be answered, because it takes you, step by step, through all the different aspects of the situation.

When Tarot Readings Fail

Believe it or not, sometimes -- no matter how hard you try -- it's just impossible to get a good reading for someone. There are a variety of reasons for this, and it's not as unusual as you may expect. Here's what to do if it happens to you.

Make Your Own Tarot Cards

So may be you're someone who doesn't want to buy a deck - perhaps you haven't found one you like, or nothing you see really resonates with you. No worries! Many people get crafty and creative and make their own Tarot cards. Here are some suggestions to keep in mind if you're making your own deck.

Tarot Readings and Moon Phases

Do you have to wait for a specific phase of the moon to do your Tarot reading? While you don't necessarily have to wait - especially if you've got an urgent matter at hand - let's look at some reasons why people choose particular lunar phases to do different types of readings.

Using Tarot Cards in Spellwork

Ever wonder if you can use Tarot cards to cast a spell? You sure can - it just takes some familiarity with the cards and their meanings. Here's a guide to get you started.

Congratulations!

You've finished your six-step Introduction to Tarot study guide! By now, you should have a good grip on not only the cards and their meanings but also how you can read them. Take some time each day to work with your Tarot deck, even if you only have time to pull one card in the morning. Try to read not only for yourself but for other people.

If you've found this study guide useful, be sure to check out our Introduction to Paganism Study Guide, which includes thirteen steps to help you build a foundation of basic Pagan knowledge.

Remember, Tarot reading is not "fortune telling" or "predicting the future." It is a tool for introspection, self-awareness, and guidance. Use your cards each day, and you'll be surprised at the depth of information they will reveal to you!

II. Get tarot ready as beginner

Although the common belief is that tarot cards are meant to tell the future or reveal someone's fortune, this is actually far from true. In contrast to this belief, tarot is a valuable form of meditation on the present moment that returns valuable insight and advice.

It will enable the person receiving the reading to connect to his or her inner wisdom and help to understand what he or she needs to know about a particular situation. It will give insight to past, current and future events based on the person's current path at the time of the reading. The cards will determine the best course of action based on what is known and what the cards show.

1. CHOOSE YOUR TAROT DECK

One of the main ways to get a good start with tarot reading is to choose a good deck. There is an old tale that you shouldn't buy your first tarot deck, but that it must be given to you. Unsurprisingly, according to tarot experts, this is very much a myth. Actually, it's "just a silly superstition and bullocks," says intuitive reader and author Theresa Reed: "It's the surest way to get a deck you don't like. Or to be kept waiting." So drop that notion right now and shop your heart out.

But, you should still go into the process mindfully. You want to find a deck that resonates with you and your tastes because you're going to work with the deck and will go back to it over and over again.

The good thing is that there are thousands of tarot decks with so many different backgrounds, you can find a deck that's perfect for your personal needs and desires. Examine the decks as carefully as you can. What is your first reaction to the images? Do you like colors and patterns? Do to the images and the artwork attract you? Are there other variations of the deck that are more appealing? If you are holding it, how does it feel in your hands? Can you handle and shuffle them easily?

Best Beginners Deck

Besides the aesthetic and physical feel, you should also consider your own experience level and learning method. Most beginners opt for the Rider-Waite deck or the Thoth deck. These two decks have rich symbolism – which allows for both classical and unique interpretations for a deep understanding of the subconscious and there is a huge amount of information available as beginner books and websites refer to these decks most often. One of my personal favorites is the Tarot the Marseille deck. This deck is considered to have been developed in Italy, it was introduced into France in 1499. The artwork was created by using woodcut techniques and colored by hand.

Still unsure which deck to work with? Together with the Tarot Association and thousands of experienced tarot readers we created a list with the top ten decks for beginners.

2. FAMILIARIZE YOURSELF

After you've purchased a deck, the first thing to do is to familiarize yourself with the cards. This probably will take some time, as the deck contains 78 cards, which are divided into two sections, the Major Arcana, and the Minor Arcana. All the cards have different meanings. In addition, you have to learn how the cards interact with each other. According to Holisticshop learning to read the tarot cards is like learning a new language. "You begin by studying individual cards, as you would learn individual words. You then become aware of how the cards in a spread interact, which can be compared with learning to put words together to form sentences. As you practice speaking a new language you become familiar with its nuances and notice how different inflections can change the mood of a sentence."

The most given advice to beginners is to do a daily card pull where you pull one card from the deck. Before pulling the card, it's good to have a question in mind. You have to avoid questions that can be answered with a yes or no. Instead, use questions that will put the responsibility back on you. What can I do? How can I take personal action? Look at the imagery and think about the meaning of the card. Decide what the card would mean when you pull it in a spread. If you do this in the morning, you can keep it in mind as you go through your day. That's a nice way to get to know the cards on a deeper level, which will result in better readings.

3. SLEEP WITH A CARD UNDER YOUR PILLOW

According to the celebrity tarot reader, Angie Banicki sleeping with a card under your pillow will also help you to get to know the cards. "Pull a card and put it under your pillow at night. Let the energy of that card seep into your dreams," she said to Insider. "Wake up in the morning; observe the card. Read about what its different meanings are. Then notice during the day what happens that might have been a sign from the cards. It's pretty cool when you start connecting the messages. Once you start connecting the messages, she said, you'll soon realize that things are not happening by coincidence."

4. LEARN SOME BASIC SPREADS

A tarot spread is a layout of cards, that will give you a structure in which you can explore your questions. Each position in the spread reflects an aspect of your question to consider. You don't have to use them for every reading. It is, however, a nice way to get started while you learn about the cards.

One of the most popular spreads is the Celtic Cross Tarot Spread, which consists of 10 cards. Although it's a beautiful spread, it's not a great place to start for the tarot beginner, because of its 10 cards.

Instead, you can better use a 3-card spread that represents the past, present, and future or mind, body, and spirit of the person being read. Even a 3-card spread can give you the insights needed. Besides, it's a great and simple way to see how the cards create stories when they're placed together.

5. GOOD ENERGY

The space in which you conduct your tarot readings is incredibly important. It is what creates trust and allows to open up. Therefore you should think about the energy of the space before starting your reading. But do not only think of the physical space that needs to be in sort before starting a reading. Your mental, emotional and, spiritual spaces matter too! Make sure you create a sacred space within each one of these elements.

6. FIND A TAROT BUDDY

Every person has their own way of looking at things. That's why every reader will interpret the tarot cards differently. Therefore it can be very helpful to find a study buddy and practice reading the cards together. You can learn from each other, share your different perspectives and support each other's growth.

7. READ TAROT BOOKS

Growing and developing your tarot skills often means reading anything and everything you can get your hands on. This, however, can be a bit overwhelming. Especially when you first start out, as there are 1000's of tarot books to choose from. Where to start with so many options available, how do you know what to choose and what resonated with you? To help you, I made a list of my favorite tarot books that helped me to deepen my relationship with the cards and the tarot system.

8. HAVE FUN!

Last but certainly not least: remember to have fun while learning. When you start with reading the tarot cards, it can be overwhelming. It can seem like there is just so much to learn and figure out. But don't freak out and just try to let it be fun and easy. For example, if you go out with friends, just pull three cards that will tell you something about how things will go that evening. Let the cards decide your nights and see if the advice turned out well!

CHAPTER 3: TAROT QUOTES

1. "Remember that the Tarot is a great and sacred arcanum – its abuse is an obscenity in the inner and a folly in the outer. It is intended for quite other purposes than to determine when the tall dark man will meet the fair rich widow." — Jack Parsons

2. "It's said that the shuffling of the cards is the earth, and the pattering of the cards is the rain, and the beating of the cards is the wind, and the pointing of the cards is the fire. That's of the four suits. But the Greater Trumps, it's said, are the meaning of all process and the measure of the everlasting dance." — Charles Williams

3. "Divination is the quest to understand more about the past, present, and future. In other words, Tarot readings are an attempt to understand ourselves better and discover how we might live better in the future." — Theresa Francis-

Cheung, Teen Tarot: What the Cards Reveal About You and Your Future

4. "Tarot is a card game that you don't play to win or lose. If there is a winner, it's the player who discovers the value of play itself." — Philippe St Genoux

5. "The unknowable lives in a pack of cards after it has been fairly shuffled but before it has been dealt, when all the possibilities are open, and when each possibility matters." — Steven Burst and Emma Bull

6. "We tarot lovers tend to be the sensual sort. We trade in shadow and gloom because we are willing to brave the literal and figurative darkness." — Sasha Graham, Tarot Experience

7. "…animal imagery [is] an important reminder to listen to nature and seek guidance in her voice rather than relying

entirely on the cold intelligence of man." — Siolo Thompson, The Linestrider Tarot

8. "A good Tarot Reader never gives false hope or leave a client feeling disturbed." — Leslie Anne Franklin

Although similar in some ways, tarot and astrology both have their differences. While astrology is calculable and closely related to mathematics, tarot's essence comes from its freedom of interpretation, which depends on each reader. However, with so many interesting facts about both astrology and tarot, there is no wonder that their practice still lives till this day.

9. Tarot reveals hidden truths.

"Fear is dangerous, not the tarot. The tarot represents the spectrum of the human condition, the good, the evil, the light, and the dark. Do not fear the darker aspects of the human condition. Understand them. The tarot is a storybook about life, about the greatness of human accomplishment, and also the ugliness we are each capable of." – Benebell Wen

10. Tarot is timeless.

"It is the province of the tarot reader to move backwards, forwards, even sideways in time." — Sasha Graham

11. Tarot requires you to connect with your inner self.

"Tarot Reading is an art based on intuition, interpretation, and perception." — Nikita Dudani

12. Tarot is meant to be used as a personal tool.

"Tarot Card are the best friend you can ever have. They are always there for you." — Nikita Dudani

13. Tarot gives guidance but you still have free will.

"Tarot Cards are your guidance cards." — Nikita Dudani

14. Tarot is about the journey, not the end result.

"In every deck, the Fool is in a precarious position. Think of all of the idioms we have for taking chances. "Going out on a limb." "Winging it." "Break a leg." "Going for broke." These all sound really painful, but what they're about is deciding that being still is not for you. When you see this in a reading, you'll know it's time to jump." — Melissa Cynova

15. What you see in the Tarot is within you.

"You are the Secret. Let Tarot Explore you." – Shweta Tarot

16. A reading will last a lifetime.

"This is your karma. You do not understand now, but you will understand later. The source of pain is within your own larger expression of being." — H. Raven Rose

17. Tarot is for everyone.

"That kind of swagger. The "I got this" energy. That's the Magician. You see this card a lot with successful people, or with people who've just found the correct path in their life and have just had that Eureka! moment. He's President Barack Obama backed by the P-Funk All Stars. Just sit down, kiddo. He's got this covered." — Melissa Cynova

18. Tarot is evolving.

"Books are like Tarot decks. They provide answers and guidance but more importantly, they are doorways and portals to the otherworld and the imagination. They leave their imprint and keep whispering to us long after we close the pages or shuffle the deck." — Sasha Graham

READY TO START YOUR TAROT JOURNEY?

Learning how to read tarot cards is an incredible journey that gives you valuable insight and advice. While it's a fun pastime, do not be fooled! You'll discover that tarot is more than a parlor game. Especially when you start to speak the tarot language fluently – including the nuances and different inflections – you'll realize that things are not happening by coincidence.

So, let's get started, buy a deck that resonates with you and start to practice. Stick to simple spreads, simple meanings, and simple techniques. You'll find your confidence grow immensely when you keep it simple. Ow and… don't forget to enjoy the journey!

Please feedback to me about this book from you!

Printed in Great Britain
by Amazon

47571212R00050